Penguins vs. Puffins

★ Julie Beer ★

NATIONAL
GEOGRAPHIC
KiDS

Washington, D.C.

Contents

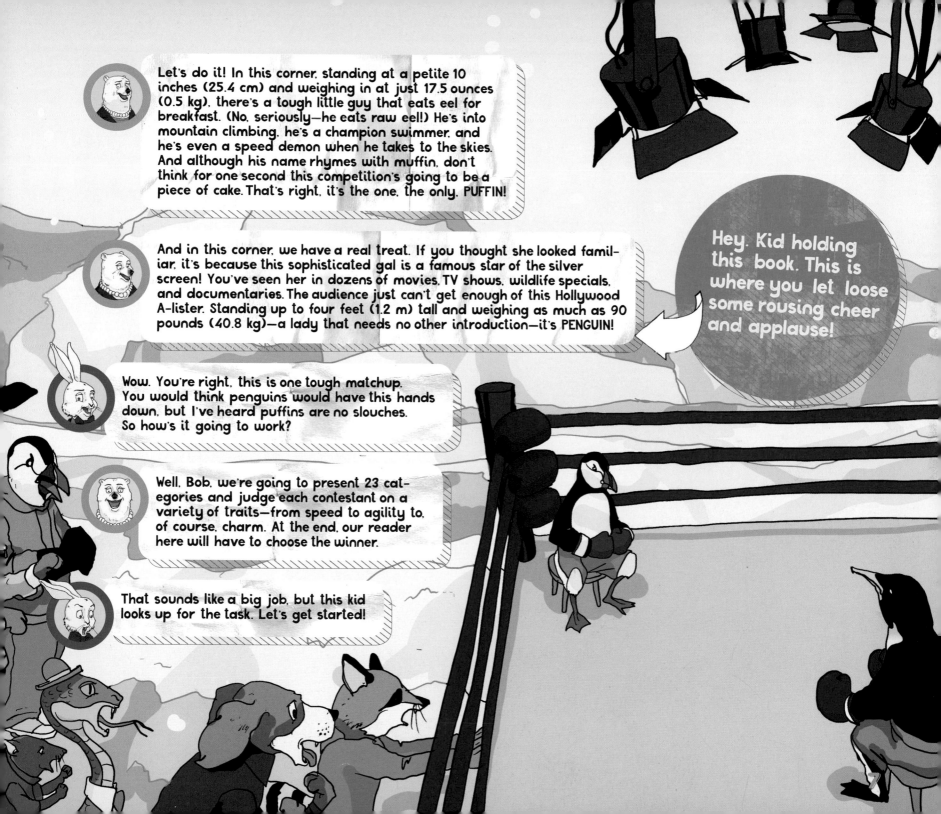

Meet the Contenders

Before we jump into the ring, let's take a moment to say hello to our opponents!

PUFFINS

Dive-bombing in from the Northern Hemisphere, we have three adorable species of PUFFINS. There's no question, these "sea parrots" are ready to take on their seabird rivals in this epic battle of awesomeness!

Atlantic

horned

tufted

PENGUINS

And next we have ... Whoa! It looks like the penguins brought a lot of friends to this showdown! Did somebody yell "fowl?" Have we already got ourselves an unfair match? All right, all right ... let's take a look at what the puffins are up against. Waddling in from the Southern Hemisphere, we have 17 dapper species of PENGUINS!

Let the throwdown begin!

Adélie

African

chinstrap

emperor

Fiordland

Galápagos

gentoo

Humboldt

king

little blue

macaroni

Magellanic

rockhopper

royal

erect-crested

Snares

yellow-eyed

OK, now you've had a look at both teams. Do you already know which one you're rooting for? Are you sure? Think you can be swayed to the other side? Well, let's just see if you have the same opinion after we present some fierce battles!

Battle of the Biggest

OK, let's clear the air on something we've all been thinking: At first glance, penguins and puffins do sort of look alike. They both possess what appears to be sophisticated charm with their black and white "dressed-for-the-ball" formal feathers. (Hey, they don't call tuxedos "penguin suits" for nothing!) But besides their formal getups, they're actually totally different in just about every way, including their size. Put puffins and penguins back-to-back, and—we hate to say it, folks—there's a clear winner.

Birdbrain fact
IN GENERAL, THE LARGER PENGUIN SPECIES HANG OUT IN COLDER CLIMATES (THINK ANTARCTICA), WHERE THEIR SIZE GIVES THEM AN ADVANTAGE IN THE CHILLY CONDITIONS. SMALLER PENGUINS PUT THEIR WEBBED FEET UP AND LOUNGE WHERE IT'S WARM AND SUNNY, LIKE AUSTRALIA.

Penguins

Does bigger mean better? Well if it does, then this battle is a bust! Of all the penguin species, the biggest daddy of them all is the emperor. It stands about as tall as a six-year-old kid! Now, not all penguins are as slam-dunk-ready as the emperor. Little blue penguins, found in Australia and New Zealand, are a quarter the size of Antarctica's local emperor. And coming in at only three pounds (1.4 kg), those little blues are serious lightweights compared to their cousins to the south!

Puffins

Atlantic puffins are about as tall as the jug of milk you use to pour on your breakfast cereal. And they weigh about as much as a can of soda. (Horned and tufted puffins are just a tiny bit bigger than their Atlantic friend.) So it's true, penguins and puffins aren't exactly nose-to-nose, or, er, beak-to-beak, in the height department. But c'mon. Does the biggest always win? Team Penguin might argue it does, but let's check out a few more categories. After all, this throwdown has just begun!

emperor

Atlantic

HEY, who you calling short?!

Well this is a throwdown, and we have to call it like it is.

Best Turf

ARCTIC OCEAN

NORTH AMERICA

EUROPE

ASIA

ATLANTIC OCEAN

PACIFIC OCEAN

AFRICA

Equator

PACIFIC OCEAN

Galápagos Islands

SOUTH AMERICA

INDIAN OCEAN

AUSTRALIA

ANTARCTICA

Where puffins live

Puffins

If you're still having trouble telling the difference between a puffin and a penguin, don't worry. There is zero chance you'll ever have an awkward run-in with them both at the same time in the wild. Why? They don't live in the same place! Puffins live north of the Equator and penguins (except for the Galápagos penguin) live in the south. In fact, besides zoos and aquariums, there is not one place on Earth that you can see a penguin and a puffin hanging out together! So which bird occupies the best real estate? Let's find out!

Want to go play with the puffins? Well, pull out your scarves and mittens because puffins prefer to chill out where it's mighty nippy most of the time—think Alaska, Iceland, Maine, and Canada. But for much of the year, they're simply floating out at sea, gobbling up fish and tidying their feathers. It's not until breeding season that they fly ashore. For a long time, no one really knew Maine's Atlantic puffins' secret winter fishing spot. Then in 2016, scientists solved the mystery and discovered they hunker down off the coast of New York! Well this playdate just got interesting!

Atlantic

12

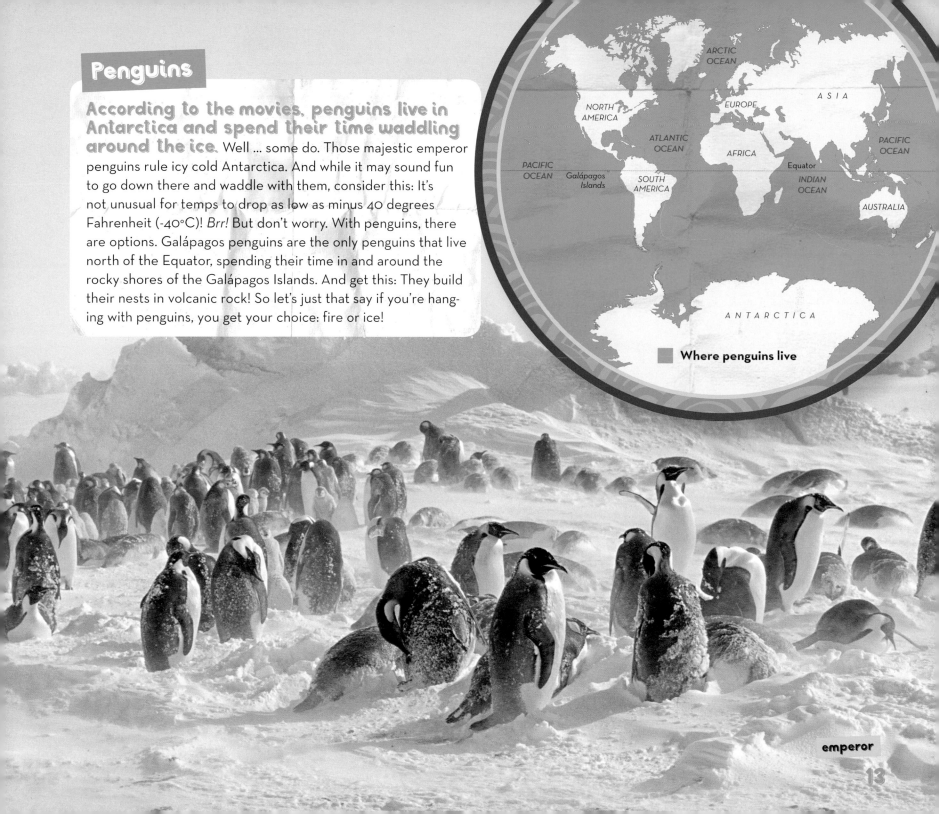

Penguins

According to the movies, penguins live in Antarctica and spend their time waddling around the ice. Well ... some do. Those majestic emperor penguins rule icy cold Antarctica. And while it may sound fun to go down there and waddle with them, consider this: It's not unusual for temps to drop as low as minus 40 degrees Fahrenheit (-40°C)! *Brr!* But don't worry. With penguins, there are options. Galápagos penguins are the only penguins that live north of the Equator, spending their time in and around the rocky shores of the Galápagos Islands. And get this: They build their nests in volcanic rock! So let's just that say if you're hanging with penguins, you get your choice: fire or ice!

ARCTIC OCEAN

NORTH AMERICA

EUROPE

ASIA

ATLANTIC OCEAN

AFRICA

PACIFIC OCEAN

PACIFIC OCEAN

Galápagos Islands

Equator

SOUTH AMERICA

INDIAN OCEAN

AUSTRALIA

ANTARCTICA

Where penguins live

emperor

Best Dressed

Black and white are always chic, but it's the bling that's the tiebreaker in this challenge. A puffin "nose" that a splash of color can make an outfit pop. And let's just say certain penguin species have some hair-raising getups.

rockhopper

Penguins

The only accessory a penguin really needs is a bow tie, but some species mix in their own special something. Take the macaroni penguin: A long crest of yellow and orange feathers flows from its head like eyebrows gone haywire. Eighteenth-century British explorers thought the feathers on these guys looked like the "macaroni feathers" found on men's hats at the time. (You know the song "Yankee Doodle"? "He stuck a feather in his hat and called it macaroni." Those are the macaroni feathers we're talking about!) And then there are rockhoppers: Just imagine taking the extravagant macaroni and adding hair gel. They too have punk-rock yellow feathers on either side of their eyes, but in between they have a mohawk of black feathers that sticks straight up!

Puffins

Rudolph has his red nose, Pinocchio has his long nose, and puffins ... Get a look at those beaks! Taking a cue from Paris fashion shows, puffins wait until spring to bring out their flare. (During the winter, the color of their beaks—and feet—fade to a duller color.) While Atlantic puffins have brilliant orange grooved bills, horned puffins' signature style is the black "horn" lines that point upward from their eyes. Tufted puffins take it up a notch with blond feathers that flow off the back of their crown. Puffins may be shy, but their look is loud!

Strut your stuff!

tufted

horned

15

Highest Flier

OK, puffins. This is your moment to shine. Puffins can win any flying competition, while penguins ... well, they simply flop and flap!

Puffins

Puffins don't just fly, they soar.
They can speed through the sky as fast as a horse can sprint on a racetrack! Sure, their pear shape doesn't scream "aerodynamic," but their rapid-fire wings—reaching up to 400 beats per minute—become a black blur while they barrel in from sea toward land. While these jet-setters are quick, their cruising altitude is low—an average of just 30 feet (9.1 m) above the sea. Takeoff, however, is sometimes a bit of a challenge. If they've just gorged on a mouthful of fish, that full belly really weighs these lightweights down, making liftoff a little bumpy!

Atlantic

Penguins

Unlike other birds, penguins have solid bones (like yours). Guess what that means? Zero flying ability! Modern penguins' ancestors once flew, but over time their wings evolved and became rigid, like flippers, better suited for swimming and catching fish underwater. Plus, denser bones made them less buoyant so they could dive deeper to snatch those fish. So while penguins can "fly" through the water, you won't ever seem them surfing air currents in the sky. However, there is one exception! They are such powerful swimmers that when they zip out of the water to burst onto ice, they are airborne for almost a full second! You call that a flightless bird? Well, yeah, it is. But it's still impressive!

emperor

Birdbrain fact
PENGUINS ARE THE ONLY BIRDS THAT CAN'T FOLD THEIR WINGS!

Best Swimmer

Ooh, this is going to be a tough one! Both of our competitors are very comfortable in the water. We now know that puffins rule the skies, but they pack the one-two punch of being formidable swimmers as well. But then there are penguins—those footballs with feet were designed to be in water! You gotta figure they know a thing or two about swimming. Let's see which one of these birds makes the biggest splash in the sea.

emperor

Penguins

Penguins were engineered for ocean life. Tip a penguin on its side and it's round in the middle and pointy at the ends—the perfect little torpedo for gliding through water. Their flipper-like wings give them plenty of power, and those short feet may be goofy looking on land, but underwater they are little rudders that help them navigate their way to dinner. Most penguins can cruise underwater at speeds between four and seven miles an hour (6.4 to 11.3 km/h), but the gentoo would sweep the Penguin Olympics. Its top speed is 22 miles an hour (35.4 km/h)! Not too buoyant and not too heavy, penguins can cruise through the water as effortlessly as most birds sail through the sky.

Puffins

Uh-oh. Those penguins seem to have a wing up in the swimming department. But don't flip out just yet: Puffins don't exactly need a set of water wings to get around. Let's not forget that unless they're nesting, puffins spend their life out at sea. Here's the cool thing about puffins: When they swim underwater, they look exactly like they're flying in the sky! Whizzing along at about three miles an hour (4.8 km/h), they pump their wings and glide as effortlessly as they do above water. And like penguins, they use their feet to steer themselves to their next meal.

Atlantic

Coolest Playground Name

PUFFBALL!
SEA PARROT!
PENGY!
WADDLER!

Boy, you've got to have thick skin to be a penguin or puffin! Let's see who rules the roost in the nickname department.

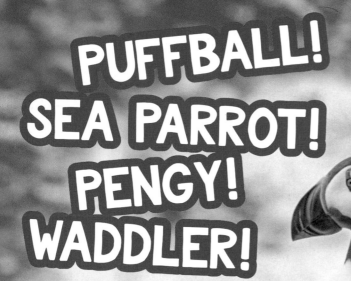

Atlantic

20

Puffins

The name "puffin" likely comes from the word "puff," which fits the bill—they are little puffs with a big beak at one end and bright feet at the other. Of course, many people call them "clowns of the ocean" because of that festive neon orange-yellow beak. Others call them "sea parrots"—again, because of the beak. Puffins' scientific genus name is *Fratercula*, which means "little brother" in Latin. "Little brother" refers to their black-and-white markings that look a bit like a friar's robes. That's all pretty good stuff, but you won't believe this: A baby puffin is called ... a puffling!

Too cute!

emperor

Penguins

Oh boy. That bar has been set mighty high. Well, baby penguins are called chicks. Makes sense. They're birds after all. Hmm ... well, when penguins gather to breed it's called a rookery or (better yet) a penguinery. *Aww.* A group of penguins in water is called a raft. Now that's clever! Can you guess how chinstrap penguins got their name? Yep, that little black line across their neck looks like the chinstrap to a helmet. Penguin polo, anyone?

Happiest Feet

Penguins waddle across ice and puffins hop on rocks. There's no question, both of these birds know how to use their webbed footsies to get the job done. But for the purposes of this battle, we must ask: Which one is lighter on their feet?

Puffins

When puffins aren't bobbing out at sea like apples in a barrel, they are hanging around some pretty steep rocky cliffs. These little mountain climbers don't need a harness or rope—their orange feet have sharp nails that do just fine navigating the terrain. Puffins forgo flying to hop and duckwalk to and from their burrows when they aren't gazing out at the sea.

horned

Penguins

Believe it or not, those short little penguin legs were made for walking! Emperor penguins walk some 50 miles (80 km) to their breeding site in Antarctica every year. Short legs + long walk = slooooow going. Their pace—1.7 miles an hour (2.7 km/h)—is about half the speed of yours when you're walking at a quick clip. Penguins' legs and feet are positioned to the back of their body, which helps give them that perfect posture. (The next time a grown-up tells you to sit up straight, pretend you're a penguin and you'll be set.) The color of a penguin's feet depends on the species—some are black, some are orange, and some are even pink!

Birdbrain fact
PENGUINS THAT LIVE IN COLD CLIMATES ARE CONSTANTLY STANDING ON ICE AND SNOW. TALK ABOUT COLD FEET! WHY DON'T THEIR FEET FREEZE TO THE ICE? FOR STARTERS, COLD-WEATHER PENGUINS HAVE FEATHERED LEGS TO HELP CONSERVE HEAT. PLUS, THEY HAVE ARTERIES IN THEIR LEGS THAT ADJUST BLOOD FLOW DEPENDING ON HOW COLD THEIR FEET ARE. THIS KEEPS THEIR TOOTSIES TOASTY LIKE WARM FUZZY SLIPPERS!

gentoo

Best Parents

There are perks to having a puffin or penguin as a mom or dad. For starters, you don't have to get out of bed for breakfast! If you're a penguin chick, you're served nice, warm regurgitated fish. That's right, food that Ma and Pa already ate, then brought back up and dribbled right into your mouth. Delish? Hardy pufflings get a nice raw fish dropped at their feet from Day One. Yum! Let's take a look at penguins' and puffins' individual parenting styles to see which one wins the trophy for best mom and dad.

Atlantic

Birdbrain fact
PUFFINS DIG A SIDE BURROW ESPECIALLY FOR BATHROOM BREAKS—A PUFFIN PORTA-POTTY!

Puffins

To prepare for their little puffling, puffin parents dig a burrow, or tunnel, several feet long on rocky cliffs and line it with feathers and grass. Mama Puffin lays one egg, then both parents take turns keeping it warm. But get this: Instead of sitting on their egg, puffin parents tuck the egg under their wing and lean on it. Puffins are obviously cuddly, but who knew they were snugglers, too? Once Baby Puff is born, the couple rotates flying out to sea to snag some fish for themselves and their little one. Puffin couples often stay together their whole lives, reuniting at the same burrow site every year.

Penguins

Emperor penguins take a similar tag-team approach to parenting. After trudging the equivalent of two marathons (50 miles/80 km) to their breeding site, Mama Penguin lays a single egg, then makes a quick and delicate handoff (make that "footoff"—penguins don't have hands!) to Papa, who will stay with the egg for the next several months while the missus waddles up to 50 miles (80 km) back to the sea. Mama will bulk up on food for herself and, of course, bring some back up for Pengy Jr., who oftentimes will have hatched while Mama was off on the hunt. Emperors don't build a nest. The egg balances on Dad's feet and is covered by his "brood pouch," a feathered flap of skin that keeps the egg warm. Once Mama shows up, there's little time for hugs and kisses. Papa, who hasn't eaten for four months, quickly passes off their bundle of joy so he can trudge off to fill his growling belly.

Some penguins do build nests. Adélie penguins line their nests with small rocks!

emperor

25

Cutest Baby

Hey there, folks! Wow, I have to say, this battle is really heating up! I don't know about you, Bob, but I'm getting whiplash going back and forth from Team Puffin to Team Penguin.

No kidding! I'm flip-flopping like a fish out of water! This seems like a good time to take a pause and check in with our special correspondent, Franco, for an in-depth look at our feathered foes' beginnings—back when they were wee little ones freshly cracked from the egg.

Thanks, Bob! Ah, yes, if you think penguins and puffins are cute now, you're going to melt when you hear about their adorable upbringings. Let's start with this cute little emperor penguin. This fuzzball is 100 percent Daddy's girl. When she peeked out of her egg, her mom was off hunting for fish while her dad's fuzzy brood pouch kept her warm and cozy. She would stand on top of his feet to keep her tootsies from getting too cold. Isn't that the cutest thing?

I think we can all agree her fluffy feathers were totally adorbs, but sadly they weren't waterproof. That meant she had to wait awhile until she could take a dip in the Antarctic waters. All that standing around looking cute can get a little boring, so when she was up for it, she waddled over and mingled with the rest of the penguin colony. She quickly learned that a penguin pack is way better than hanging solo—less chance of those pesky skua birds swooping in and trying to snag her! Eek!

Get ready for the feel-good moment: Before too long, good ol' Mom showed up from her long walk back from the sea.

emperor

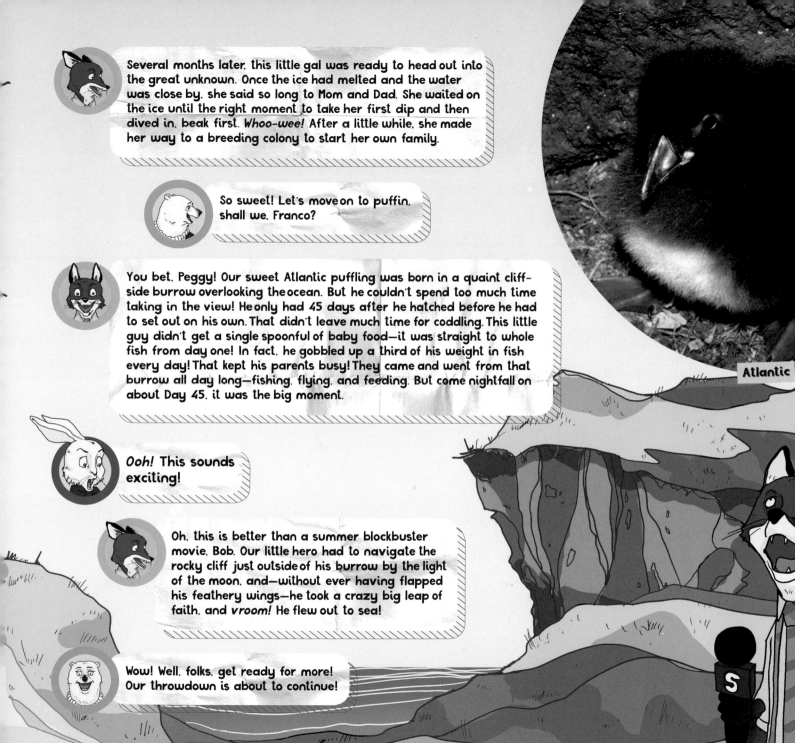

Several months later, this little gal was ready to head out into the great unknown. Once the ice had melted and the water was close by, she said so long to Mom and Dad. She waited on the ice until the right moment to take her first dip and then dived in, beak first. *Whoo-wee!* After a little while, she made her way to a breeding colony to start her own family.

So sweet! Let's move on to puffin, shall we, Franco?

You bet, Peggy! Our sweet Atlantic puffling was born in a quaint cliff-side burrow overlooking the ocean. But he couldn't spend too much time taking in the view! He only had 45 days after he hatched before he had to set out on his own. That didn't leave much time for coddling. This little guy didn't get a single spoonful of baby food—it was straight to whole fish from day one! In fact, he gobbled up a third of his weight in fish every day! That kept his parents busy! They came and went from that burrow all day long—fishing, flying, and feeding. But come nightfall on about Day 45, it was the big moment.

Atlantic

Ooh! This sounds exciting!

Oh, this is better than a summer blockbuster movie, Bob. Our little hero had to navigate the rocky cliff just outside of his burrow by the light of the moon, and—without ever having flapped his feathery wings—he took a crazy big leap of faith, and *vroom!* He flew out to sea!

Wow! Well, folks, get ready for more! Our throwdown is about to continue!

Biggest Celebrity

Look, there's not a single puffin or penguin with a star on the Hollywood Walk of Fame, so no one should get too boastful here. However—bird bias alert!—the penguins do kinda win this one hands down. Whoops! We mean, penguins have a lot of experience with fame.

Penguins

From splashing around Mr. Popper's bathtub to dancing their way through *Happy Feet*, penguins are powerhouses at the box office. And hello, *Madagascar*! The sneaky penguins were such a hit in that movie they got their own spin-off, *Penguins of Madagascar*. Sorry, puffins, it gets worse: The penguins even have a video game based on the movie, and there was a *Penguins of Madagascar* TV series! And let's not forget, penguins can be serious actors, too. In 2005, they were the stars of the documentary *March of the Penguins* and—this is going to hurt, Team Puffin—they won an Academy Award. Ouch!

emperor

Puffins

Well this is awkward. Um, well, a puffin played a major role in *Happy Feet Two*. You know, Sven, who everyone thinks is a penguin that can fly but he's actually a puffin? (See, there goes that penguin-puffin confusion again!) Besides that, puffins have their face on a breakfast cereal called, what else? Puffins! So while penguins may win big at the movies, puffins go better with milk! (Wait, that doesn't sound right ...)

Atlantic

Class Clown

Uh-oh, penguins! You're in hot water for this competition. A puffin's nickname is "clown of the ocean"! How are you possibly going to win the category of "class clown"? It's going to take a red honker nose, a rainbow wig, and oversize shoes to win this battle!

Puffins

If this were a costume contest, the puffins would win by a nose. Just hand them some balloon animals and puffins are ready to entertain at any kid's birthday party. But puffins aren't just clown look-alikes—they play the goofy part as well. For instance, we all know one of the best clown tricks in the book is the fake, clumsy fall down, right? Puffins have that nailed! Except ... it's not fake. When puffins come in for a landing, stay clear! Those little pears wobble and bobble until they plunk themselves down, and sometimes it's with a thump! (And if the landing is in the water, it's with a splash!)

Atlantic

Penguins

A penguin's costume may be stuffy and serious, but this bird certainly knows how to cut loose and have a clownishly good time. Like this: When cold weather penguins get tired of doing their little penguin shuffle, they plop on their bellies and go for a slide on the ice! This playful move is called—what else?—tobogganing! And better yet, they use their wings and feet to steer. High marks in the silly category, penguins. But they have another trick of the trade: Adélie penguins can be found lining up on icy cliffs, taking turns diving into the ocean below, then climbing back out and diving again! Sounds like this act is ready for the circus!

emperor

Birdbrain fact
PENGUINS CAN GLIDE ON THEIR BELLIES FOR MILES AT A TIME! THAT'S ONE LONG SLIDE!

31

Most Photogenic

Penguin selfie! #cutepuffin! If penguins and puffins were on social media, they'd have more followers than a pop star. Check out these snapshots and decide whether penguins or puffins are better at mugging for the camera.

#squadgoals
JUST A LITTLE
CHEST-PUFFIN.

#fashionista
DOES THIS MATCH
MY OUTFIT?

#bedhead
I WOKE UP LIKE THIS.

#twinning
UNPLANNED MATCHING OUTFITS!

#openwide
DO I HAVE FISH BREATH?

#followme
I KNOWS WHERE ALL THE GOOD FISH IS.

#smooches
KISSING PARENTS—SO AWKWARD.

Best Diver

No scuba gear required: Penguins and puffins have superb underwater diving skills to help them find their next meal. But while both of these birds can take a deep dive when necessary, only one qualifies as a full-time mini-submarine.

Puffins

Think you can hold your breath longer than a puffin?
If it must, a puffin can dive underwater to hunt fish for up to a minute, but most dives last just 20 or 30 seconds. Here's the thing: They can dive as deep as 200 feet (61 m) in that one minute! That's as deep as the Leaning Tower of Pisa is tall! That's no Pisa cake!

Atlantic

Penguins

Hey, puffins! Emperor penguins can dive 1,850 feet (565 m)—that's deeper than One World Trade Center, the tallest building in the Western Hemisphere, is tall! They can dive deeper than any other bird. And don't even try to compete with penguins in a breath-holding contest: They can stay underwater for more than 20 minutes! How do they do it? Well, those solid bones help them sink, plus they have heavy muscles.

emperor

Scariest
Archnemesis

Seriously, who in the world would ever want to hurt a cute little penguin or puffin? Well, for every hero there's a villain, and some villains have an appetite for adorable birds. Boooo! The question is, which of our heroes has the scariest villain that they must fend off?

Penguins

It's a good thing penguins are such good swimmers because they sometimes have to make some quick getaways underwater. Leopard seals, sharks, and orcas all have a taste for penguins. On land, adult penguins don't have a lot to worry about, except for predatory birds—like great skuas and giant petrels—that like to snag baby chicks. Ack! Galápagos penguins have to fight off foxes and snakes that try to snatch their eggs, which they lay in caves or holes of volcanic rock. Sweet penguins turn sour when predators attack, but since penguins don't pack a punch, the odds are stacked against them.

gentoo

Puffins

Puffins can't catch a break! They have predators on land and in the air. Enemy Number One is gulls. The great black-backed gull can snag a full-grown Atlantic puffin in midair. Then on land, herring gulls lurk, waiting for puffins to return with a mouthful of hard-earned fish, and then steal it from them! Even worse—and you might want to cover your ears for this one—the gulls will seek out puffin burrows to try to steal eggs! Tufted puffins not only have to fight off snowy owls and bald eagles, but arctic foxes, too. Foxes like to sneak up on puffins, which is why the clever puffins hang out on steep cliffs that can be too hard for four-legged creatures to navigate.

Atlantic

Look out, puffin!

Biggest Chatterbox

We want to know what the puffin and penguin have to say! Puffins look so shy. Are they going to be able to take on those sassy penguins? Put on your earmuffs, because this battle is going to get LOUD!

Puffins

Puffins are the picture of serenity when standing on cliffs. All is quiet and serene; you can hear the waves crashing, but there's not a peep from those puffins. But that's above-ground. Inside those burrows, puffins let loose! Puffin parents make a growling noise that sounds like a chain saw, or a squeaky door! That's not the only sound they make. When a puffin couple is building their nest together, they often pause to tap on each other's bills. This is called "billing," and in puffin talk it means, "Hey, partner! You're with me!"

Atlantic

Penguins

The question isn't, What sound does a penguin make? It's, What sound do a thousand penguins make? When all those penguins gather in their penguinery, or breeding spot, you'll be looking for a volume control button because they have things to say! Surprisingly, penguin couples somehow find a way to tune out all that noise and zoom in on their mate. Even after months apart, they find each other by calling out. What sounds like a honk! honk! to us is, "Hey, Polly! I'm over here!" to a penguin.

Does anyone have a pair of earmuffs? It's LOUD in here!

king

Most
Graceful

In a showdown of poise and grace, who is lighter on their feet? Put on your swim goggles because that puffin coming in for a landing is about to make a splash! And whoa there, little penguin! You might need to put on some hiking boots to steady those feet!

#faceplant
WHERE ARE THE ICE SKATES WHEN YOU NEED THEM?!

#wipeout
WHEN A GAME OF HEADS OR TAILS GOES BAD.

#incoming
YOU'VE BEEN WARNED!

Let's Try That Again ...

Now there's a stately looking penguin. A picture of charm and sophistication. And what is that puffin pondering? Poetry, perhaps?

#mygoodside
SHOULD I MAKE THIS MY PROFILE PIC? Y OR N?

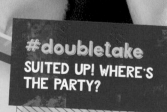

#doubletake
SUITED UP! WHERE'S THE PARTY?

#TBT
TO THAT TIME I HAD THE ROCK ALL TO MYSELF.

#nofilter
THE ICE IS NICE DOWN SOUTH!

#spoiled
SERIOUS PARENTAL GUIDANCE!

Best Meet and Greet

OK, we are well into this epic battle. And by now surely you've shouted over to your parents, "Can we go see a puffin?" (Whoops, bird bias alert! "Can we go see a penguin?") Penguins and puffins can, of course, be found in all sorts of zoos and aquariums around the world, but let's think big here. What if your parents OK'd a vacation to visit a puffin or penguin in their natural environment? Which one lives in the coolest travel destination?

gentoo

Penguins

We know that some types of penguins can be found in Antarctica. Yes, it's a haul to get there, but finding the penguins is relatively simple, especially if you head to the heart of the Antarctic Peninsula at Port Lockroy. You don't have to pull out your binoculars or ask the locals for the best viewing spot. Just head straight for ... the post office! No, penguins don't arrive there by airmail (Helloooooo! Penguins can't fly!), but a colony of 3,000 gentoo penguins have made the post office at Port Lockroy their breeding grounds. Cruise ships come ashore here in the summer and tourists drop off postcards at the post office, and then snap photos of the penguins—including newborn chicks. The Port Lockroy post office has gentoo penguins' stamp of approval—why not yours, too?

Puffins

You can't just walk up to a post office in puffin territory and expect to see a puffin. That's not the way puffins roll! But where they live is an easier journey than trekking to the gentoos in Antarctica! Head to New Harbor, Maine, U.S.A., between mid-May and late August and jump aboard a Puffin Watch cruise that heads to Eastern Egg Rock—a famous puffin stomping ground. Trips leave in the late afternoon, which is prime puffin-spotting time, and on this trip you will need binoculars! Remember, puffins are little guys, so you'll need to scan the water and Eastern Egg Rock to spot a sea parrot, but many ships also have a naturalist aboard who's on the lookout and will provide expert information and tips. Of course, by now you're an expert, too!

Atlantic

Weirdest Talent

Boy, this matchup is a real nail-biter! It's so close, the tiebreaker might just come down to which one of these goofballs has the craziest special talent. So c'mon, penguins and puffins, show us your wackiest tricks!

Puffins

Get this: Those little puff-balls can hold not one, not two, not 22, but as many as 62 fish in their beak at once! Whaaaaat? That's insane! The average mouthful is a mere 10 fish, but one Atlantic puffin in Britain was spotted holding 62. This trick definitely needs a "don't try this at home" disclaimer. However, puffins have special tools to help them hold on to all that food: Their tongues are designed to hold fish up against the spiky spines on the roof of their mouth. (Basically, they can Velcro fish to their palate.) With the fish firmly gripped, they can catch more fish. Talk about biting off more than he could chew!

Atlantic

emperor

Penguins

A Velcro mouth that can hold 62 fish! You'd have to be a magician to top that. But penguins have a few tricks up their sleeves as well—like, say, a built-in bubble machine in their "tuxedo." Let's explain: So we know penguins can't fly, but they can swim fast underwater and then come bursting onto land. They're certainly not using a pool ladder to jump out of the water, and probably not a water cannon, so how are they doing it? Just before they become airborne, penguins release air bubbles from their feathers that form a coat of bubbles around them. Getting rid of that air reduces drag, letting them double their speed for a split second to achieve their dramatic entrance onto the ice. Sure, it ends in a belly flop, but isn't it worthy of a round of applause?

Biggest Magnet
for Scientists

Scientists are trying to learn more about penguins and puffins—to find out about their habits and to help their populations thrive. But puffins and penguins aren't too keen on scientists hanging out too close. So scientists are pulling out all kinds of gadgets and trickery to get the job done!

Penguins

It looks like every other penguin chick—fluffy and adorable. But wait! Why is it rolling? That's no penguin—that's a robot! (OK, technically it's a rover.) And its job is to infiltrate the colony and collect data. It's Spy Penguin! Chick cam, as it's called, was immediately accepted into a colony of emperor penguins, and the rover captured a mama penguin laying an egg—something that had never been captured on film before!

emperor

Puffins

Before there were rovers, puffin scientists were tricking puffins, but with something simpler and without wheels: wooden decoys. Because of overhunting, by 1969 there were only two breeding colonies of Atlantic puffins left in Maine. Ornithologist Stephen Kress and his team of "puffineers" lured puffins back to their historic home on Eastern Egg Rock, off the coast of Maine, in part by putting up wood puffin look-alikes. Puffins fell for it, and even tried tapping bills with them. (The puffins' getting-to-know language.)

Psst! I think it's just a disguise.

Atlantic

Best Table Manners

Penguins and puffins may live at opposite ends of the globe, but their menu is quite similar: fish—for breakfast, lunch, and dinner. Yum! Fish smoothie, anyone? Let's see which bird has the most munchable menu.

Penguins

Those speedy penguins have no problem catching a fish underwater, but who doesn't want a little variety? Depending on where they live, penguins will also snack on squid and crustaceans, including krill, a shrimp-like animal. Penguins don't need to worry about chewing with their mouths closed because they don't chew! They catch their prey in their bill and their spiky tongue keeps it from slipping away. Then they swallow it whole!

Humboldt

Puffins

Quick! Hide the sushi! Puffins love raw fish. But they aren't picky eaters. Some of their other favorite foods are sand eels, herring, and hake (a type of cod). They often eat their food on the go, right after they catch it, but you can also spot puffins on land with a mouthful of fish spilling out of their bill. Talk about fish breath!

Atlantic

Ultimate Survivor

If puffins and penguins were on a reality TV show of survival, both would definitely make it to the final round. Emperor penguins' everyday life is tough already—they have that epic long walk to lay and care for their eggs, plus they have to outswim leopard seals! Puffins can't ever let down their guard: They have to worry about being attacked in the sky and on land! But that's just the beginning. Both penguins and puffins face dangers they have very little control over.

Atlantic

Puffins

Puffins look cute on paper, but historically people prized puffin feathers as decorations on their hats, and even used their feathers to fill pillows. Overhunting is what caused the puffin colony on Maine's Eastern Egg Rock to disappear. Oil spills by tankers or drilling can cause puffins to lose the waterproofing on their feathers, putting them at risk in cold waters. And in some parts of the world, especially Iceland, puffins are often ... dinner! Smoked and sautéed, puffins have been the "national dish" of Iceland for hundreds of years.

Penguins

Penguins and puffins both face threats, but there is one piece of good news for penguins: While people once hunted penguins and collected their eggs, both practices are now illegal. But penguins are also at risk from oil spills; plus, commercial fishing has reduced the number of fish in some penguin breeding areas, which means there isn't always enough left for the penguins to catch. In Antarctica, melting sea ice, due to climate change, has meant the loss of habitat for penguins.

king

Most Amazing Adaptation

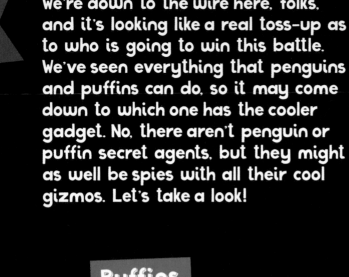

We're down to the wire here, folks, and it's looking like a real toss-up as to who is going to win this battle. We've seen everything that penguins and puffins can do, so it may come down to which one has the cooler gadget. No, there aren't penguin or puffin secret agents, but they might as well be spies with all their cool gizmos. Let's take a look!

tufted

Puffins

Swallowing ocean water not only makes your lips feel puckery—if you drink too much, it can make you sick. Not a problem for puffins! Puffins have special glands above their eyes that filter saltwater and release the salty stuff through the puffins' nostrils. Supercool gadget! But it gets better: Puffins have their very own built-in swim goggles! OK, not exactly. They have an extra eyelid that allows them to see better underwater! (Plus, it protects their eyes from injuries.) Every cool spy needs a cool outfit. Puffins have what's called countershading (they're white on their chest and black on their back), a form of camouflage that makes them harder for predators to spot. Bring it, penguins! What do you have to show us?

Penguins

Well, as a matter of fact, penguins also have that fancy gland that filters saltwater. And they have the third eyelid, too! So there! And countershading? Check! Got that, too! So, um, when it comes to the battle of cool adaptations, puffins and penguins end in a draw!

gentoo

55

Decision Time

 Well, Bob, that was one tough battle!

 No kidding, Peggy. Just when I thought the penguins had it, the puffins would swoop in with something crazy-cool.

 Crazy, cool, and cute! I mean, "puffling"? Adorable!

 And give it up for those penguins. Did you see that fluffy chick hanging out with the robot? That was pure penguin perfection.

 It sure was! I'm so glad I'm not the one judging this contest! So, do you think this kid here has made a decision?

 Hmm, let's ask. Hey, kid! This is the big moment. Drumroll, please! Who have you chosen? Should we have a quick recap?

Puffins Replay

Height: 10 inches (25.4 cm)
Weight: 17.5 ounces (0.5 kg)
Number of species: 3
Range: North of the Equator
Flight speed: Up to 55 miles an hour (88.5 km/h)
Swim speed: About 3 miles an hour (4.8 km/h)
Diving depth: 200 feet (61 m)
Favorite food: Fish
Greatest enemy: Gulls
Known for: A clownish beak

Penguins Replay

Height: Up to 3.8 feet (1.2 m)
Weight: Up to 90 pounds (40.8 kg)
Number of species: 17
Range: Mostly south of the Equator
Flight speed: Zero
Swim speed: Up to 22 miles an hour (35.4 km/h)
Diving depth: 1,850 feet (565 m)
Favorite food: Fish, squid, and crustaceans
Greatest enemies: Leopard seals and predatory birds
Known for: Starring roles in blockbuster films

Quiz:
Are You a Penguin or a Puffin?

In your heart of hearts, are you a penguin or a puffin? Take this quiz to see if you're more penguin or puffin-like!

1 Do you have a fear of flying?
A. Yes
B. No

2 When you get ready for school, do you ...
A. focus on getting your hairdo just right?
B. make sure you have just the right accessory to accent your outfit?

3 How long can you hold your breath?
A. More than 20 seconds
B. Less than 20 seconds

4 Which of the following best describes you?
A. You take loads of selfies and group photos with friends.
B. You'd rather stand behind the camera and take the photos.

5 Which would you rather do?
A. Go for a hike.
B. Go rock climbing.

If you mostly answered A, welcome to the club, Pengy!
If you mostly answered B, you've joined the circus, Puffin!

Next Up:
Explore More About Penguins and Puffins!

You've learned loads about penguins and puffins, but this is just the tip of the iceberg! Check out these resources to keep exploring and learn how you can help them!

WEBSITES

The Cornell Lab of Ornithology: All About Birds
allaboutbirds.org

Audubon Project Puffin
projectpuffin.audubon.org

Project Puffin Visitor Center, Rockland, Maine, U.S.A.
projectpuffin.audubon.org/visit-us/project-puffin-visitor-center

National Geographic Kids: Atlantic Puffin
kids.nationalgeographic.com/animals/atlantic-puffin

Puffin Loafing Ledge Cam
explore.org/live-cams/player/puffin-loafing-ledge-cam

Defenders of Wildlife: Basic Facts About Penguins
defenders.org/penguins/basic-facts

National Geographic Kids: Emperor Penguin
kids.nationalgeographic.com/animals/emperor-penguin

National Geographic Kids: Adélie Penguin
kids.nationalgeographic.com/animals/adelie-penguin

National Geographic Kids: Humboldt Penguin
kids.nationalgeographic.com/animals/humboldtpenguin

California Academy of Sciences: Live Penguin Cams
calacademy.org/explore-science/live-penguin-cams

BOOKS

Davis, Lloyd Spencer. *Smithsonian Q & A: Penguins: The Ultimate Question & Answer Book.* Harper Perennial, 2007.

Kress, Stephen W. *Project Puffin: How We Brought Puffins Back to Egg Rock.* Tilbury House Publishers, 2003.

Schreiber, Anne. *National Geographic Kids Readers: Penguins.* National Geographic Kids Books, 2009.

FILM

March of the Penguins. Warner Bros., 2005.

HELP PROTECT PUFFINS AND PENGUINS

ADOPT-A-PUFFIN

projectpuffin.audubon.org/get-involved/adopt-puffin

ADOPT-A-PENGUIN

https://secure.defenders.org/site/SPageNavigator/
wagc_penguin.html

gifts.worldwildlife.org/gift-center/gifts/
species-adoptions/emperor-penguin.aspx

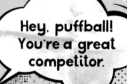

Hey, puffball! You're a great competitor.

Index

Photo Credits

Illustrations throughout by Michael Byers.

FRONT COVER: (LE), Nancy Elwood-Naturesportal/Getty Images; (RT), Franka Slothouber/Minden Pictures; **BACK COVER:** (LE), David Yarrow Photography/Getty Images; (RT), RandyRimland/Getty Images; **BACK FLAP:** (UP), Anton_Ivanov/Shutterstock; (LO), mlorenzphotography/Getty Images

INTERIOR: THROUGHOUT (background), LilKar/Shutterstock; 1 (CTR), Makc/Shutterstock; 2 (LE), Christian Kober/Getty Images; 2 3 (RT), Frank Krahmer/Getty Images; 3 (RT), Life on White/Getty Images; 3 (LE), Steve Allen/Getty Images; 4 (CTR), Frank Krahmer/Getty Images; 8 (RT), Theo Allofs/Minden Pictures; 8-9 (background), jolly_photo/Shutterstock; 8 (CTR), GlobalP/Getty Images; 8 (CTR CTR), DESIGN PICS INC/National Geographic Creative; 9 (CTR), Gerard Lacz/Minden Pictures; 9 (UP CTR), Franco Banfi/Minden Pictures; 9 (UP CTR), Eric Sohn Joo Tan/Minden Pictures; 9 (LO), Nigel Pavitt/Getty Images; 9 (LO), Marco Simoni/Getty Images; 9 (LO), Richard Siday/Getty Images; 9 (LO), Westend61/Getty Images; 9 (UP), J & C Sohns/Getty Images; 9 (LO), Sue Flood/Minden Pictures; 9 (CTR), Ole Jorgen Liodden/Minden Pictures; 9 (LO), Rinie Van Meurs/National Geographic Creative; 9 (UP), TUI DE ROY/National Geographic Creative; 9 (UP), Jason Edwards/National Geographic Creative; 9 (CTR), Frans Lanting/National Geographic Creative; 9 (LO), Shannon Hibberd/National Geographic Creative; 9 (UP), Ralph Lee Hopkins/National Geographic Creative; 9 (CTR), Frans Lanting/National Geographic Creative; 11 (RT), Life on White/Getty Images; 11 (LE), Steve Allen/Getty Images; 12 (CTR), Fritz Poelking/SeaPics.com; 13 (CTR), Joseph Van Os/Getty Images; 14 (CTR), Martin Priestley/Getty Images; 15, Matthias Breiter/Minden Pictures; 15 (background), Skillzman/Getty Images; 15, Gary Schultz/Getty Images; 16 (CTR), Nancy Elwood/Getty Images; 17 (CTR), Paul Nicklen/National Geographic Creative; 18 (CTR), Paul Nicklen/National Geographic Creative; 19 (RT), Glen Bartley/Getty Images; 19 (LE), Paul Nicklen/National Geographic Creative; 19 (CTR), Alex Mustard/2020VISION/Minden Pictures; 20 (CTR), Flip De Nooyer/Minden Pictures; 21 (CTR), Stefan Christmann/Minden Pictures; 22 (CTR), Marie Read/Minden Pictures; 23 (CTR), Paul Souders/Getty Images; 24 (CTR), Andrea Thompson Photography/Getty Images; 25 (CTR), Stefan Christmann/Minden Pictures; 26-27 (background), designelements/Shutterstock; 26 (LO LE), Frans Lanting/National Geographic Creative; 27 (UP RT), Mike Jones/Minden Pictures; 28 (CTR), Tui De Roy/Minden Pictures; 28-29 (background), alphaspirit/Shutterstock; 28 (CTR CTR), AF archive/Alamy Stock Photo; 28 (RT), Everett Collection, Inc.; 28 (LO CTR), Everett Collection, Inc.; 29 (LE), Nancy Elwood-Naturesportal/Getty Images; 30 (CTR), Mike Lane/Getty Images; 31 (CTR), Daniel J. Cox/Getty Images; 32 (RT), Rhinie van Meurs/Minden Pictures; 32 (LE), Daisy Gillardini/Getty Images; 32 (LO), mlorenzphotography/Getty Images; 33 (UP LE), Hiroya Minakuchi/Minden Pictures; 33 (LO LE), David Yarrow Photography/Getty Images; 33 (UP RT), Carl Court/Getty Images; 33 (LO LE), Arthur Morris/Getty Images; 34 (CTR), Barcroft Media/Getty Images; 35 (CTR), Paul Nicklen/National Geographic Creative; 36 (CTR), Paul Souders/Getty Images; 37 (CTR), Bjoern Backe/Alamy Stock Photo; 38 (CTR), Cyril Ruoso/Minden Pictures; 39 (UP RT), Gordan Court/Minden Pictures; 39 (CTR), Nathalia Michel/Getty Images; 40 (CTR LE), Klein & Hubert/Nature Picture Library; 40 (LO), David Tipling/Getty Images; 40 (RT), John_Jobling/Getty Images; 41 (RT), Klein & Hubert/Nature Picture Library; 41 (LO LE), Andy Rouse/Getty Images; 41 (UP), Mike Lane/Getty Images; 42 (LE), Julien Poirion/Minden Pictures; 42 (CTR), TUI DE ROY/National Geographic Creative; 43 (LO RT), Tui De Roy/Minden Pictures; 43 (LE), Stefan Christmann/Minden Pictures; 43 (UP), Robert Thompson/Minden Pictures; 44 (CTR), Michael Nolan/Robert Harding/Getty Images; 45 (CTR), AP Photo/Robert F. Bukaty; 46 (CTR), Frans Lanting/Getty Images; 47 (CTR), Paul Nicklen/National Geographic Creative; 48 (CTR), Nature Methods/Nature Publishing Group; 49 (CTR), AP Photo/Robert F. Bukaty; 50 (CTR), gerard Lacz/Visuals Unlimited/Getty Images; 51 (CTR), Avalon/Photoshot License/Alamy Stock Photo; 52 (CTR), age fotostock/Alamy Stock Photo; 53 (CTR), Yva Momatiuk and John Eastcott/Minden Pictures; 54 (CTR), Otto Plantema/Minden Pictures; 55 (CTR), Paul Nicklen/National Geographic Creative; 56 (LE), Theo Allofs/Minden Pictures; 56 (RT), Richard Siday/Getty Images; 58 (LO), Fritz Poelking/SeaPics.com; 58 (LE), Martin Preistley/Getty Images; 58 (LO RT), Alex Mustard/2020VISION/Minden Pictures; 58 (UP RT), Paul Nicklin/National Geographic Creative; 59 (LO RT), Doring Kindersley/Getty Images; 63 (RT), Eric Isselee/Shutterstock; 64 (LE), Fredy Thuerig/Shutterstock; 64 (RT), ullstein bild/Getty Images

Thanks, Pengy. You're not so bad yourself.

To my daughters, Katie and Leah, who first spotted puffins with me in Alaska. —Julie Beer

Since 1888, the National Geographic Society has funded more than 12,000 research, exploration, and preservation projects around the world. The Society receives funds from National Geographic Partners, LLC, funded in part by your purchase. A portion of the proceeds from this book supports this vital work. To learn more, visit natgeo.com/info.

NATIONAL GEOGRAPHIC and Yellow Border Design are trademarks of the National Geographic Society, used under license.

For more information, visit nationalgeographic.com, call 1-800-647-5463, or write to the following address:

National Geographic Partners
1145 17th Street N.W.
Washington, D.C. 20036-4688 U.S.A.

Visit us online at nationalgeographic.com/books

For librarians and teachers: ngchildrensbooks.org

More for kids from National Geographic:
kids.nationalgeographic.com

For information about special discounts for bulk purchases, please contact National Geographic Books Special Sales: specialsales@natgeo.com

For rights or permissions inquiries, please contact National Geographic Books Subsidiary Rights: bookrights@natgeo.com

Designed by Eva Absher-Schantz
Illustrations by Michael Byers

National Geographic supports K–12 educators with ELA Common Core Resources. Visit natgeoed.org/ commoncore for more information.

Hardcover ISBN: 978-1-4263-2869-5
Reinforced library binding ISBN: 978-1-4263-2870-1

Printed in Hong Kong
17/THK/1

The publisher would like to thank National Geographic Kids editor Ariane Szu-Tu and National Geographic Student Expeditions leader Justin M. Bowen for inspiring the idea for this book, and everyone else who helped make this book possible: Christina Ascani, associate photo editor; Gus Tello and Anne LeongSon, design production assistants; and Alix Inchausti, production editor.